KT-442-941

REMINISCENCES OF NORMA

Also by Martin Seymour-Smith

Poetry

Poems, with Terence Hards and Rex Taylor
Longmans (Dorchester), 1952
Fantasy Pamphlet No. 9, Fantasy Press, 1953
All Devils Fading, The Divers Press, 1954
Tea With Miss Stockport, Abelard-Schuman, 1963
U.S.A: Barnes & Noble

Satire

The Bluffer's Guide to Literature, Wolfe, 1966; U.S.A: Cowles

Criticism

Robert Graves, British Council (1956), revised 1965
Fallen Women, a study of the prostitute in literature,
Nelson, 1969
Poets Through Their Letters Vol. 1, Constable, 1969; U.S.A: Holt,
Rinehart & Winston
Inside Poetry, with James Reeves, Heinemann, 1970;

Editions

Poetry from Oxford, Fortune Press, 1951
Shakespeare's Sonnets, Heinemann, 1963; U.S.A: Barnes & Noble
A Cupful of Tears, Wolfe, 1965
Every Man in his Humour – Ben Jonson,
New Mermaid, Benn, 1966; U.S.A: Hill & Wang
A New Canon of English Poetry, with James Reeves,
Heinemann, 1967; U.S.A: Barnes & Noble
Poems of Andrew Marvell, with James Reeves, Heinemann, 1969

Martin Seymour-Smith

REMINISCENCES OF NORMA

Poems 1963-1970

CONSTABLE
London

First published in 1971 by
Constable & Company Ltd
10 Orange Street London WC2

ISBN *0 09 457190 2*

Printed in Great Britain by
Western Printing Services Ltd, Bristol

TO SALLY CHILVER

La Pasionaria, *what's permitted?*
What is grace? The communists all want Ben-
Ville Manor. No pasaran. *But they did.*
They do. Oh now what really does go on
In your head (what sadness turned it grey?)
Throughout the purpose-ridden Russian day?
If I did not talk too much I'd listen
To all the things you wisely would not say.

CONTENTS

I SATIRES

II THREE IMITATIONS

IV OTHER POEMS

I
SATIRES

THE INVITATION

Toupée askew after the dusty journey
He stepped blinking out onto the platform
And she was there to greet him.

They had said in the blurb (he wrote it)
'Himself a poet and critic of distinction';
So nice it had been to receive her letters –
Almost unbelievably naïve they were:
'I'll send a photograph so you can recognize me' –
And to be invited to her flatlet
Before lecturing to a local thought-group.

After the photograph he'd indeed taken interest,
With its accompanying note:
'Love in your more than tentative estimation
Is exactly what I too have been searching for;
Men here are coarse in comparison to what you have said;
What Krishnamurti suggests, you are . . . .'
He was rubbing his hands, he could not help it
(Though properly ashamed).

So now, belly held back, with springier step
Than at P.E.N. or Hampstead parties,
He strode down the platform.
'So this is Westcliff . . .'

And she was even better than he had expected, hanging on to
His every word like an angel.

Soon, with whisky's special sincerity, he was saying:
'The spirit is everything but I have a habit
I have struggled with all my life.
You can talk about it with me. Give me advice.

I think physically, need to discuss
The ethereal significations
Comfortably between sheets, with someone like you.
Whatever happens
It would be different with you.
The contact would scarcely matter.'

Then, when apparently safe in her bathroom,
Having a wash and brush-up before immediate bed-work,
Regumming his wig, whistling with appreciation,
Lower plate riding firmly on the shrunken gum
The door burst open.
Youths,
Reckless and sharp in shiny jackets with emblems, healthy at twenty,

Knocked him down, kicked his soft underbelly;
Stamped on him as if he'd been Coriolanus –
While brazen in her shift she stood and smiled:
'I shall eat these two in a jiffy, Mr. Poet.
Take their blows as my advice.
Crawl back to the Smoke. Two can play
At your game – and don't forget it.'

And limping from Fenchurch Street, pubs not yet open,
Clutching his shredded corset,
Hair pocketed in the too-stiff breeze,
He realized that for the first time ever
He was helplessly, generously, forgivingly,
In hopeless love;

And he read with joy in an Essex newspaper how
He had been taken suddenly ill
And Miss Love herself had deputized with a talk on
Aspects of poetry.

QUEEN LEER

Sado-pathic, thanks for drawing
Some madness out of me.
Forgive me now that I am throwing
You through sewers to the sea:
Successful poultices grow more than grey
When hoarded past their one half-day.

CENSOR JACK

In his rare spasms does Censor Jack shout out
The words he rules that we must do without?

SUNDAY MORNING WALK

Trapped as the Church disgorges
Its pollarded congregation
I note the bred not-glance
Of a fascicle, which forges
By variform configuration
Autonomy's *insouciance,*
At an unholy ostentation
(Disciplined intimation
Of next week's battered sermon):
My Russian failure to enhance
Sunday's achromatic orgies
By ritual excoriation
Of my face. Oh Christless ignorance!
Nor does this growth, though getting on for
A *Light-of-the-World*-ish length
Imply the kind of moral strength
That could empty a Church with scourges.
No. But noon's nasty shadow's more
Scissile, when an encumbrance,
Than weeds whose ravages suggest
That beardless integration
Is no remedy at all for plants.

I HAVE NEVER FELT

'I have never felt that there was any inherent virtue in powerful feelings and simplicity, though evidently some poets . . . Poetry can be honest, I agree, but it has greater duties . . . it must perform its moral functions. . . . I don't enjoy poems written by . . . wastrels.' – J. Fuller, *Poetry Society Bulletin 60*, 1969.

Upon men of unfortunately strong emotións,
Moral failings
And vile simplicity
Is ever-fixéd the most baleful, disapproving gaze
Of Fuller, J., versificationist,
And teacher of the young, of Magdalen, Oxenford.

I plead to you: observe unease. You're not enjoyed.
Spit out those siren tears.
Eat your proper bloodless meat
Oh wastrel Mariner:
Life's troubled bubble's broke by John.

When he encounters problems domestic
John's feelings are, I hope, 'not strong':
He life's greater duties knows
And's more agreeable.

May on the public map of Poesy
O rally-hard his driving be:
Directions planned, and navigator-uttered
With superb correctitude;
All watches synchronized, and face
Set in determination quite as strong
As your foul feelings are.

And learn from John, meanwhile, your grief to minimize
Should he not win.

THE CRUEL GRAVY

I used to be a stanzaic boy, conned the porters at Christchurch, used quaint words, scanned the swans at the edge of the sedge, pernoctating. Now i am concreto purely, though there were stages: pour example i had a period cool in streatham i penned structures for analysis notrelated to my self, a promisung organic persona notexisting a structuremaster from wch big Wimsatt cd extract i rhymed it big, was winning whn without warning a friend said that « shatskin » wd be giving a strong talk at the Penge Ethicallogueinthechair It changed my *vida*POETRYhesd quotinghis banne d address to the workers of Omsk / IS THE DIRTYVEST u cast off after labour: :THAT & MY WIFE'S CON crete knockers/ /endofshatskin / I am not read but the freedom of these massesappeals;s.wentwithaMercedes into the river but had given me the beginning / SERIOSO mes amis i am now one of you UUU ChristLogue Spike Jack am out to SHOCK SHOC K i will use FEAR LESS WORDS mein freud i am bearded now PERFORM SMELL am in ADVERTISING &my lines honour MY breathingnotthe sense. That crazyShakescene was *projective*plusfield compostit's better now & i can still astonishingly hv a sherry with dons 'mongst silvertheyto me listen somewith davy I mopwithbreadpellets up gravy pity applauding me armpits & i will give you th clothes next me skin * INTIMATE? goodby!] ½tomlinsong wightman polyfilled flute] E

THEY LIKE GRAVY

TO ALL WATCHERS OVER PUBLIC MORALITY

Secret dwarf pornographers who live
In your cisterns, repressed gentlemen,
Gaze lewdly at you as you bath.
What a heavy burden you have to carry!
They are yourselves,
The utterances you have banned:
They pen long nasty books and peddle them,
Sure of sale (true offspring of your commission)
In the rusty Paris of the pipes. . . .

Here you get the raw material
From which you learn your duties
To the public. Study them closely
To reach the heart of obscenity:
Long lists of bad words every schoolboy knows
(Read them aloud in the echoing bathroom as relief
To so much protocol);
But most of all pore lovingly over
The luscious glossy series showing
Policeman, truncheon and naked writer. . .

You more than weekend in dirt.

TO ALL WATCHERS OVER PUBLIC MORALITY

[illegible]
In your [illegible] ladies and gentlemen,
[illegible]
[illegible]
There are [illegible]
The [illegible]
[illegible]
[illegible]
[illegible]

There you get the [illegible] material
From which you learn your duties
To the public. Study them closely
[illegible]
[illegible]
Read them aloud in [illegible]
[illegible]
But [illegible]
[illegible]
Policemen, [illegible] and [illegible]
[illegible]

A VERSIFIER IN PRIVATE
to Poets in Public

Dangerous in my Y-fronts
To thin-legged Harrods cousins,
Sometimes I also simulate
Evenings of undefeat.
Passing my Churchill memoirs
And well bound great editions
My six suits half in mind
And the Jermyn shirts
I bear to my roseate terrace
A careful gin
And to you Leonardina show
Although you are common
An old romance
En vers surfin, parfumé,
Telling of how once, in the unkempt world,
An imprudence flicked
With stroboscopic speed.
In its lines I celebrate
That *momentito*.
But once is enough; oh never allow
Life to seep out of
The all-inclusive filing cabinet.
Fetch me my gross of condoms,
But first: fellate.
I shall put out of mind your servitude,
Let it be lost in your deglution. But
Leonardina, I shall not be involved.
I never propose:
My concinnous spurt dissolves
All fears and loves:
I am married to death.

II
THREE IMITATIONS

FEDERICO GARCIA LORCA:
1910 (INTERVAL)

Those eyes of mine in nineteen-ten
did not see the dead buried
nor the dawn-weeper's celebration of ashes
nor the trembling heart, stranded as a sea-horse.

Those eyes of mine in nineteen-ten
saw the white wall where the little girls pissed,
the bull's mouth, the toadstool
and the secret moon which in corners lit
scraps of dry lemon in bottles' hard shadows.

Those eyes of mine! in the horse's collar;
in sleeping Santa Rosa's tortured breast,
in the roofs of love – with groaning and cool hands –
in a garden where frogs ate cats.

The attic where old dust gathers statues and moss,
boxes which store the silence of eaten crabs,
in the room where the dream came true.
My little eyes are there.

Ask me nothing. I know now that lives
when they seek out their course, meet their void:
a tragedy of leaks in unpeopled air
and in my eyes the children are dressed, not bare!

UMBERTO SABA: WINTER NOON
[Mezzogiorno d'inverno]

Just when I was still contented
(God pardon me for having said
Such a vast, appalling word), who swept
My curt joy away, so that I nearly wept?
You might say, 'A certain lovely girl
Walked past you there, gave you a smile'
– But it was a balloon, a balloon
That floated, blue against sky-blue,
When my heaven had never been so bright
As at that clear, cold winter noon:
A heaven of clouds, small and white,
Of windows blazing in sunlight,
Thin smoke from a chimney or two;
And over the scene, the divine scene,
That globe which had slipped loose
From the hand of a boy who'd been
Heedless (surely he shed some loud
Tears, in the middle of the huge crowd,
For his sorrow, his enormous sorrow,
At losing his toy?).
Between the Square and the cafe
I sat in wonder watching
At how it now rose, now fell – his joy.

FERNANDO PESSOA: POETS

[Autopsicografia]

Poets pretend
They pretend so well
They even pretend
They suffer what they suffer.

But their readers feel
Not the pain that pretends
Nor the pain that is
But only their own: that's real.

And so upon toy rails
Circling reason like an art
Runs round the model train
That's known by the name of heart.

III
REMINISCENCES OF NORMA

1

I smooth out a map of where you live,
Run my finger along your street,
Feel your will in the fibre of the sheet;
But remember you said, 'I hate home:
It is so far to come';
And wishing to spare you, even in my
Helpless thoughts, from dwelling again here,
My eyes roam to the surrounding district –
Quiet villages you might have visited
In sad escape; or to which, in a dream-life,
We might have gone. But my life's not full enough
For me boldly to know such other places. . .
Defeated, I put away the map.
Find it has a cutting edge:
Has become, with the sharpness
Of your mastery, cold, and cruel.

2

It is well for you tonight pretty girl
To put on your dancing stockings and twirl twirl
In exquisite clubs of drink and lust
While I rack myself with jealous thoughts
Of brute sailors smirking
And your crushed self finding in their tattooed arms
More sweetness than in my foolish love.

Or perhaps an ambitious clerk,
The facets of his face gleaming in subdued light
Is at this moment subjecting you
To an expensive obscene ritual
From which your joy in his concentration
(Which excludes you completely),
Excludes your lover.

Or perhaps you are seducing someone comically,
Whom 'you quite like really', in a taxi:
A sick columnist who lives on pills
And celebrates, rolling naked to Wagner,
The supremacy of white rulers.

Or perhaps in teenage coffee-bars
With black discs in front of your eyes
You are committing welfare;
Yearning later to taste their contempt
And to be robbed of your awful love –
A mystery in which your lover has no share.

So in my imagined bitterness,
I, who have no rights over you whatever,
And who abuse you with such thoughts,
Jealously writhe.

Yet how can I believe
That when you take down your hair
And come to me smiling
Your heart is not there?

3

The new girl with violent hair
Ignored me daily on the stair
Her glance-away was like a stare
I make my own disasters

Across the sky I saw her hand
A bundle into a waiting hand
I wanted not to understand

Parcelled cock to be sacrificed
To a God who'll take away a life
I had not known could be sacrificed

She went down a darkening street
With a knife to make my last defeat
Who was she going that night to meet

I lay in wait for my own death
Expecting to hear my final breath
I dreamt and watched them plan my death

I saw them work at their Black Arts
Hated their understanding hearts
In the temple where death starts

But when I woke this vision cleared
I looked for the new girl whom I'd feared
The death was that she'd disappeared

Have you seen a hole in emptiness
Where nothing was have you seen less
When you feared death have you been death
You make your own disasters

4

Pasty, with brazen curls, you dream away
Your captain day:
Unblossoming you shed your right to pray.

I canker you, my bore and stride
Are cruel. Writhed in your side
I see your other face, in patience skied. . . .

As I am sickness, so you are my rose:
Even what is dying grows, and grows.
What will be what I lose

But one larger rosebud to explore?
But I promised before
Kindness, the sunned quiet of a slow shore,

Patience like yours. Then give me now,
Make me demand, that sharp rosary
To count for you, to clack endlessly
Your general time away;
Oh let me beg, cocoon at last, to be
Your sadder suffering face below –
Loathed in my lair, so skilled and grey.
By counting your scentless beads in such a way

Might not I then become
The whole true tree of you, and dragon home?

Pray, with broken [illegible], you dream away
Your captain day:
Unblossoming, you shed your right to pray.

I ponder you, my bare [illegible]
A [illegible]. Wrapped in your side
I see your other face in patience set [illegible]

As I am vehement, so you are my rose.
Even what is dying grows and grows.
What will be what I lose

But [illegible] to [illegible]
But I promised before
Sundress, the summer quiet on a slow shore

Patience like yours. Then give me now
Make me demand that [illegible]
To count for you, to black endless
Your general time away.
Oh let me hope, reckon at last to be
Your sudden stilt, the face below
Cradled in my lap, so skilled and grey
By counting your small beads in such a way

Might not I then become
The whole true tree of you, and [illegible]

5

Come with me to Heligoland. It's now
A wilderness, I think. Was bombed so often
That there's nothing there. . .

Where is it then? you ask.
Do not tease me with your map.
It would be new in this way, that there are
No night-clubs, no chance bars
Where I might embitter myself, falling
Into soft new company.

There are birds maybe; and in my dreams of you
Might be love-avoided-as-it-should-be:
The thing not in eyeshot, the lived-in beauty.

Do not wonder that now
I drum my heels against the timbers
Of a narrow passage, suspended from a hook.
This is no game I play in place of metaphor:
Remember your joking hand so long ago
That hoisted me from ground too hard to bear,
To this lowest hook my folly could hang me by?
Now I wish to celebrate you
In most barren Heligoland, where nothing's for pleasure

For beneath my feet, to rest them.
You place volumes of poetry
Who do not care for poetry.

6

Yesterday I took you to a place
And waited in the car. Now lying here in bed
I am still there: cannot remember
Returning ever. When memory fails
Today is bled, yesterday fed.
In the night with trees around I am afraid.
Let me get out of this.
What is Norma's face
And why's
The house she entered locked?
Sitting in the car's being nowhere;
Late and alone, no breath, I think no thought;
Look down at the hole in my chest, no pain, just a lump of
Blood-ice.

Many lives have I such:
Of terror – and perhaps
Sweetness indescribable?
In one I sit here, not-dead –
But in one more, amazed,
Am warm and saved.
Too much too much!
Not strange I twitching inhabit
A greyness of brains racked,
Remember not to forget.

Yesterday I took you to a place
And visited in the car. Now lying here in bed
I can still see each one in my mind,
[illegible] ever. When morning's [illegible]
Today is black [illegible]
In the middle with trees around I am afraid
For me and only [illegible],
[illegible] spring light
And [illegible]
The [illegible] entered upon
[illegible] in the car being nowhere
Late and alone, [illegible], I think no thoughts
[illegible] down in the hole in my chest, [illegible]
[illegible]

Many fled from Europe:
[illegible]
[illegible]
In one [illegible]
But in one [illegible]
And [illegible]
[illegible]
[illegible]
[illegible]
[illegible]

7

I met you, Norma, dearly young,
In scented night. Though you spoke of wars
Between men and women, of alternate triumphs,
I noticed the trees only, ghostly-green
In dark. Your youth excited my mind,
My eyes were fixed, I did not dare to think
So much for your embrace I longed.
You were so fair
You would not lead me home until sun shone.

The flies were busy round desire
Before you drew me in. I eyed
The crossed dildoes on your walls,
The sex-stained trophies
The splendid images of death;
In my own first gruntings heard the buzzings of decay
On the tender face of that amorous day;
Wanted to stay.

I tried to be decent in our sty;
Found pleasure gave
Sense back to my eye:
While you lolled into rest
I saw that you were older than I thought
And knew you as a witherer of green,
Obscene
And rotting Helen of all wars never won.
Yet for passion I strained on:
Your stench was that of the divine.

Now you are silent I miss your mind,
Lack the stink of your vanished rind.
Oh how long in your palace will I lust alone
For bones whose flesh so long ago I wronged?

8

Bring Norma
                    was a phrase I overheard
Put me in danger. Nothing to do with me;
But John and she did arrive in my mind's
Small cliff-perched house, cut off,
In sneering wind. Below,
The slow sea like a shapeless serpent stirred
In changing blue.
Alone for a moment, as in a fantasy. . . .
Not right of course but I thought: Oh
I want you too. Then John was dead.
We watched his body fall towards the sea.
Then murder made my sex-dreams real.
They come me now to choke, with their white hood
Put on my head.

This is not true, nor was she real, and yet
I am condemned, a felon in a net,
Nor can wake.

9

'One of the best of a valuable series. . . .'
I get bored, love, although of course it's interesting and, true;
Yes love I know that while
On helpful exegeses, dry, of hot desire
I work, you sit there still
Though I no longer quite believe in you –
Now I am so bland may not you strike
And shall I have have have
The old entire, despiséd dream?
Cor!

Nerves would be shot, I should be ill,
Flesh like you might seem.
It's true that strange
Breasts are marvellous meat
But do be wiser lust –
And you, word, in your seat,
You Norma you
Are mostly ghost.

10

Goodbye common history
there is no name
I can give that she
but yours
Norma
Wife-figure? Ma? This is a photoplay in which
I do not I hope participate
Actress, you,
Sweet in the part, so appealing, true

The theme? Some horrible actions in a park:
Worse than sex-deaths, never-seen;
An old man made appearance
On dusks of murder-nights,
Was seen through railings in the mist,
Seemed made half of stone; and half of silence

Then horror. Next night you whom we trust,
So kind, so lovable
An early Anna Neagle in an X!—
Are seen there, thighs
Tempting in the grey, a hint of breasts, but
Face softish stone spilling reckless flesh

That was not I! Sweetly said to my relief
My poor father must not seem to be
The one whose victims die. It was for him.
So noble are you, in this plot, until

I wake to find a face, half flesh and half decay
Turning to stone: this must be the dream. I say:
This is not true, Oh this is just the play

There is no play

Another communication

there is no name

I thought that [illegible]

[illegible]

Name

Who knows who. This is a photocopy in which

I've not before participated

Actors:

[illegible] in the past, a [illegible]

That tuning fork: both [illegible] tones in a garb

[illegible]

[illegible]

[illegible]

Was seen through falling in the mist

[illegible] made half of snow and half of silence

Then [illegible] man where we [illegible]

[illegible] so invisible

[illegible]

[illegible]

Remains in the gravel [illegible]

[illegible]

[illegible]

[illegible]

[illegible]

[illegible]

[illegible] half flesh and half [illegible]

[illegible]

[illegible]

[illegible]

11

No vows these days
Or wine of love-praise:
We let friendship freeze
Our old intensities.
It seemed good to be
Not in love but happy:
No lies said,
Friends in bed.
But at the heart of lust
Death pissed.
What seems fragrant
Becomes rank.
And so one look today
Made by you in play
Took my smile away.
Through our soft ease
I saw my end:
The plot, the serious men,
The one absent,
The grave open.

11

No vows these days
Or vow of loud praise:
We let friendship freeze
Our old intimacies.
It seemed good to be
Not in love but happy:
No lies said,
Friends in bed.
But at the heart of lust
Death passed.
What seems tranquil
Becomes chill.
And so one look today
Made by you in play
Took my smile away
Through our soft ease
I saw my friends:
The dint, the strange mind.
The one absent,
The grave spent.

12

I left you Norma and you died alone
In that room whose ancient pieces stopped the sun.
Then from the street towards you there crept one
To wash your body lying on our dark bed:
To sponge your thighs still filthy with my sperm
And kiss pale lips that once were red and firm.
It was the ghost of me who grieving left
At dusk: my Christ-half's turn of cheek away
From me. I could not refuse its gift

And all my lightness now is filled with pain:
As you rise in my mind, so lusty and so gay.
I left you once, but now be mine to hold,
For memory warms what only real is cold!

13

This little love-God is a shit, brown-suited,
Franco-faced, and only He knows if He knows
How He awoke to find Himself i/c affairs
Or how I found myself a witness to
His dull committee. That's what the heart
Of passion's like: a group of psycho-clerks
Considering erections' powers to lie.
Let those who love divinely see the files.

But Norma, you were there, glasses and bad clothes,
Docilely bringing papers to their sides,
Your breasts in satin, peacock-blue,
And my romantic passion was, to penetrate
The centre of your secretarial art:
Love like that aches to know what it knows only,
Or is unknowable. Our sex stank everywhere,
My words were not my own, I envied the grey God-man
Who'd had you once or twice, you tart.

Not you nor God nor His cold secretariat
Can know my journey, not of miles,
To find in nothingness the love I can.

14

This little love-God is a slut, brown-suited,
Franco-faced, and only He knows if He knows
How He awoke to find Himself à-c affairs
Or how I found myself a witness to
His dull committee. That's what the heart
Of passion's like: a group of psycho-clerks
Considering erections' powers to lie.
Let those who love divinely see the files.

But Norma, you were there, glasses and bad clothes,
Docilely bringing papers to their sides.
Your breasts in satin peacock-blue,
And my romantic passion was—to penetrate
The centre of your secretarial art.
Love like that aches to know what it knows only,
Or is unknowable. Our sex stank everywhere.
My words were not my own. I envied the grey God-man
Who'd had you once or twice, you tart.

Not you nor God nor His cold secretariat
Can know my journey, not of miles,
To find in nothingness the love I sent.

IV

OTHER POEMS

MISTRAL

She went out, for a moment, she said –
  But he lay down in the wind,
Asked it to tell him what loss it was bringing;
  And their son cried 'My father is dead'.
But he with staring eyes still lay, and ringing
The wind made words on the bells
  Which spoke in his head:
  'Tell your son that his mother has sinned
  And his father is dead.'

She stooped to him, stroked him, 'Oh do not lie there
  In the wind, come in by the fire,
The bells speak lies to part us,
  Come in from there.' But she fled in fear;
And the bells rang thus:
'He will not rise, he will not rise, unless she tells
  Where she goes in the Mistral, where,
  And the story of her whole desire
  For the wind in her hair.'

The air became still, and the words he had heard
  Became her surprise:
'Where have I been that my breath
  Comes so fast? Has the Mistral stirred
The bells to speak of death?
The wind is winged and beaked, it taps on the bells
  Always a lying word.
My son, why with such frightened eyes
  Do you stare at me, as if you realise
  That I myself am the Mistral-bird?'

THE BLUE TRUMPETER

Privately to you and while confined
In the jacket of strait circumstance
I smuggle this crude message.

Forgive me free friend if I have stifled
Your unwitting music. Demands of business
Or, I might say, all of earth's beauties,
Will perish at doom. But what is doom?

Even to me, most humble and rejected,
Dreams try to speak. But the strict mind
Censors their message. Thus 'I am alone'
Is vague at too-considered morning,
Shrugged off like an astrologer's warning.
But the message lies within: I signed
By my birth a charter saying
There are Wrongs as well as Rights of Man.

Knowing you were a master of insurance
I left you coolly. Only my dream said
That I returned in afternoon, as a
Blue trumpeter. It was not as myself,
But as a marvellous warrior, famed and scarred,
The hero only I had thought of:
So alive and throbbing white, but with
Blue spots breathing decay. Yes, like this I
Turned up in your pleasant summer garden.

'You are meant to be away, spectre,'
You said, 'but since you are here, I stand you.'
And grinning horribly, to your wife's dismay,
You warned the huge world: 'Come boy, sound that horn!'

THE LITTLE TRUMPETER

[illegible]

'I am here,' I said, 'in a dream merely:
But outside this foolish sleep
I have been here, a winged officer
Of fatal interest. And you have said
"Look, look at this masterful peaked creature
With griffin-wings! He asks impossibilities!" '
(Yes, free friend. My spite to you was myth.
You live in wider gardens now. I beg
You think of all my strictures on you as
Pseudonymous – the naked angel who,
By truth's command, your life made harsh and vile.)

So I made a strange, unearthly music.
Not one understood. And as I played
(Spotted with blue decay in your garden)
I began to wake. All meaning of this dream
Receded from me. But I remember
(Oddly in a mad dream)
How from unknown dells and hidden waters
Herons rose, and veered.

"I am here," I said, "in a dream merely,
But outside this foolish sleep
I have been here, a winged officer
Of fatal interest. And you have said
'Look, look at this unmerciful peaked creature
With griffin-wing! He asks impossibilities!'
(Yes, free friend. My spite to you was mythic.
You live in wider gardens now, I beg.
You think of all my strictures on you as
Pseudonymous—the naked angel whose
By truth's command, your life made harsh and vile.)"

So I made a strange, unearthly music,
Not half understood. And as I played,
Spotted with blue decay in your garden
I began to wake. All meaning of this dream
Receded from me. But I remember
Oddly in a mad-dream
How from unknown dells and hidden waters
Herons rose, and veered.

PATHETIQUE

Early fell to the spell of
What wrong have I done love?
Wondered with you how
Gracefully not to allow
Sense a way. Did not know
Flesh has its mind, of danger,
Whose coolness is anger.
Oh why does peace have to end?
At the blue window
Heard the hoarse fulsome call,
Saw the faceless shadow
Of you now know.

THE ANSWER

Why live at all? Absurd question.
Do not ask it. I heard
One say those words, most bitterly,
The heat of circumstance
Stifling a too-guarded mind.
Discovered it was I. Went out,
Determined in the biting day,
To kill all trace of sense. Found
Curiosity too quick; returned
To starker warmth: a naked mind.

THE ANSWER

Why live at all? Absurd question.
Do not ask it. I heard
One say those words, most bitterly,
The heat of circumstance
Stifling a too-guarded mind.
Discovered it was I. Went out
Determined in the biting day
To kill all trace of sense. Found
Curiosity too quickly returned
To starker warmth, a naked mind.

SAXELBY

I was asked to compile a Dictionary
Of Names and Places in the Works of Thomas Hardy;
Was pleased at the financial opportunity –
But found the job had been done already
Sometime earlier in the century
By a man called Saxelby.

What a dull man, I thought meanly
(Though told he did it excellently)
Actually to compile a whole Dictionary
Of Names and Places in the Works of Thomas Hardy!

Yet how can I say with certainty
That, victim of terrible vices, Saxelby,
Crippled with alimony,
Pressed by mistresses and penury,
Tensely, angrily, in a drunken frenzy,
Slogging down the busless Dorset lanes disgustedly,
Did not do it only for the money?

SAXELBY

I was asked to compile a Dictionary
Of Names and Places in the Works of Thomas Hardy;
Was pleased at the financial opportunity
But found the job had been done already
Sometime earlier in the century
By a man called Saxelby.

What a dull man, I thought; for only
(Though told he did it excellently)
Actually to compile a whole Dictionary
Of Names and Places in the Works of Thomas Hardy!

Yet how can I say with certainty
That, victim of terrible vices, Saxelby,
Crippled with alimony,
Pressed by mistresses and penury,
Tragically, angrily, in a drunken frenzy,
Slogging down the [illegible] Dorset lanes dyspeptically,
Did not do it only for the money?

IN THE MARKET-PLACE

Half-heartedly at noon in the market-place,
For the thousand-and-first time, I step forward
To assert my sovereignty. Persons, gathered
To see the King my father, ignore me. Then
The usual sneer goes up: 'It's the heir again
Making his claims!' Nevertheless, while the worst –
The thieves and lunatics and hopeless cases –
Bow slobbering at my feet, the people stay:
Something to expostulate upon at lunch
If my father does not pass this way today.

But I maintain a new silence. I dismiss
My crazy disciples, join the mob itself,
Become one of them (unrecognised of course),
Chat pityingly to them of the mad heir,
Mocking him thus: 'He's silent today, praying
To himself for yet further powers and glories.
I knew him once.'

IN THE MARKET PLACE

Half-heartedly at noon in the market-place,
For the thousand-and-first time, I step forward
To assert my sovereignty. Persons gathered
To see the King my father ignore me. Then
The usual sneer goes up: 'It's the lune again
Making his claims!' Nevertheless, while the worst —
The thieves and lunatics and hopeless cases —
Bow slobbering at my feet, the people stay:
Something to expostulate upon at lunch
If my father does not pass this way today.

But I maintain a new silence. I dismiss
My crazy disciples, join the mob itself,
Become one of them (unrecognised of course),
Chat pityingly to them of the mad heir,
Mocking him thus: 'He's silent today, praying
To himself for yet further powers and glories.
I knew him once.'

PINCHBECK

Pinchbeck, constructor of automata and other desiderata,
Inventor of the mixture of copper and zinc that bears your name
(Whose second son and namesake Christopher
Manufactured astronomical clocks, automatic penumatic brakes and patent candle-snuffers),
How many of the minikin-frenzied, parchment-faced, task-rapt, time-pressed
Acquisitive master-jewellers who now so idly cry to cowed apprentices
'Hand up the pinchbeck!'
Pause to bless your brilliant vital alloy
Of base metals counterfeiting gold
Or care for your soul
Or actualize
That very darkest moment
When crossed in love and heedless on the edge of an eclipsing scandal
You head-in-hands were driven to sob: 'What is it all for?
What can I care for any more?'

Only then could hopeless red-rimmed eyes when blankly raised discover
An alchemy that never had been more than casual
So triumphing in the retort
It made you as forgetful of your private pains
As jewellers now are careless of them in their gains.

AN OBSERVATION FOR UNVERIFIABLE RECONSIDERATION IN A GAME PERHAPS

The preliminaries to your death are
This and that: shaving, a little anger,
Pat the cat's head, write a boring letter.
Your logic can show you nothing better.

Or have in your case fantasies of love
Interfered in a serious manner?
Then we have a false though common basis
Upon which to found a 'friendship' (say)
(Or if I am a lady then you may
Express yourself in a quite different way).

Put this at its very least attractive –
You must admit that on the whole it is,
From routine deathwards-going, a holiday.
Freddy can't have all analysis, no play.

Remember, then, next time your mind must curse
This godless accidental universe,
That only lies prevent it from being worse.

THE CELLAR

The monuments had gone.
Scrolls of their stone
Floated paper-light,
Scattered, settled,
On the ended world
When I saw him first,
Black, without pity.
I am dying, he said,
I shall soon be dead.

Love is death, he said,
As he led into my known,
Needed tomb;
But you did not know,
You spoke it so;
I am dying, he said,
I shall soon be dead.

In ripening dusk I saw
Blood fall from his wound
As down steps and steeper steps
He bled.
Felt in my stiffening side
New lips, the ooze of blood.
I am your father? he mocked.
And he thrust his swelling black tongue
Between my lips as I choked
Nigger, jew, queer!

Your chamber of horrors, he said,
Opening a lost door.
Your key, he said, I am dying.
Feed your wound, lock yourself in.

THE CELLAR

The moon again had come
back to their house
the poor perfect
matter'd settled
with their [illegible] world
When I saw him first,
Hands, [illegible] and
from dying like salt,
I shall save the dead

I [illegible]
as she led into my room
Nodding [illegible]
But turned the light
You spoke it soft
I am drifting [illegible]
I shall [illegible]

In open [illegible] I came
blood fell from the rafters
A dozen steps and [illegible] stairs
[illegible]
fall in my [illegible]
[illegible]
[illegible] the [illegible]
[illegible] the [illegible] black [illegible]
[illegible] my [illegible], I climbed
[illegible]

[illegible]
[illegible]
Your [illegible]
[illegible]

You'll find her there.
I knew her, but from nowhere,
Knew the two tables there,
The two pens laid;
The paper made of stone.

I need to find what you have,
For I am kind;
I need to find what you have not,
For I am cruel.
I spoke only through my side
Despite my head's despair;
Mouth could not ask, What spear?
I turned the key inside.
Went to her there.
She swung an axe at me,
Its blade swept my hair
As she swung it up there.

I am skull and skin, flesh and hair,
She said, but I am not dead.
They are dead up there.
Nothing living flies in the air,
Nothing living inhabits the earth,
The caves are empty,
But we are living, locked here.
And when I called out, Father,
Father, God the Father,
No one soothed with there there:
I heard only his blood
Drip on the stair.

I look at the walls like dark lakes,
Tall pillars no movement shakes;

I search in vain for the source of the light.
We must, she says, record all thought,
Describe our feelings as we fight –
Until what time! I ask –
Until a time that you have bought.
I can write only, Will this wound heal
Or shall I bleed to death?

She hides her writing with her hand,
Makes signs I do not understand,
Smiles at a thought.
My wound dreams of its food,
I cannot write as I should

And the sound her pen makes
Is like the hissing of snakes.

I search in vain for the source of the light.
We must, she says, record all thought.
I rake our feelings as we fight.
Until what have I left?
Until a hope that you have bought.
I can write only With this wound lent
Or shall I lifted to death

She nods her everything with her head.
Makes signs I do not understand.
Smiles at a thought.
My wound dreams of its bed.
I cannot write as I should

And the sound her pen makes
Is like the breathing of snakes

WHY

Do I cause you to do this? Or is it
A thing clear to you, but strange?
Weather, perhaps, or the change
Of seasons? We stand in fields
And share the bleakness of an Autumn day.
I feel the new chill like comfort,
You knowing yourself, but seeming to give
All your knowledge to me – or to the day?

'How can it end again?' I ask;
But when dusk ends, and when we sit,
I think contentedly,
By the fire, you spread hands like wings:
'I am leaving you for ever.
When I return, I shall have changed.'
And if you become a bird that sings
I have to love a song I do not understand.

Oh vast and vanishing accuser,
So loving as you fly,
Through all Autumns my 'why?'
Echoes, and through all such days
As those you have been with me on.
All of them are questions
Asking, in their similitude,
Where is she now? Where did she go?

Yet did I not hear her say
'Those who truly love are not of your day
Nor can they tell of where they go
Or of how you cannot let them stay'?

TO MISS PARFITT (1934) SADLY: THIS POEM ABOUT DYING

I've had too much trouble in my life.
Why, writing those words, I went back to
An ancient kindergarten cursive.
When I cried I could not do it
Soft-breasted woolly-warm Miss Parfitt
Took me on her lap. (Now I can,
And anyway, she's old.) Yes! I want
To get away from life, say nothing of
The young magus, the all-intelligent hag
Or the demands of universal love;
There is the darkness in myself
Which for too long I've said was
Not honest to hide. Let me have less
Trouble, is what I ask. . . .

And so you, to whom I have always to speak,
Say with the smile I put on strict lips
'There'll be no poems, no answers,
No harrowing of hell without
The pain you know you want'.

I know I'm speaking to you Adversary.
Must.
Let me as usual put the sentence,
In your mouth: 'For trouble you've got
Your less and less obscure aches hinting
At dying. You always have your dying,
The wish is permanent.'

But need that be trouble?

It's what I wait for, wanting
To know.

TRANSPARENTLY SAID
[illegible]

I've had my own trouble in my time
While sorting these words I went back to
An ancient [illegible]
[illegible] I found her dead
[illegible] Miss [illegible]
[illegible]
[illegible]
[illegible] from life, nothing to
[illegible]
[illegible]
[illegible]
[illegible]
[illegible]
[illegible]

And so [illegible] I have always to [illegible]
[illegible]
There is [illegible]
[illegible]
[illegible]

[illegible]
[illegible]

[illegible]
[illegible]
[illegible]
[illegible]
[illegible]

[illegible]

It's [illegible]
To know

GIRL'S SONG

Mr Tropayoz,
Do you trim our fates,
Vendor of goodies and God?
The children love
Your white push-cart,
But your azure sweets
Burn with an icy flame
In the knowing hearts
Of lonely child and lover
Who fear tales
Of the thundering beard
That wags at hell
When you mouth the Word.

Oh monstrous heavens of my blue eyes
Let the stars in them
Trick you into another love:
If then I let you tumble me
Will you change your too vast ways,
Check the divine threat, sweetheart,
For a season be strictly mine,
So that the hopeless people,
Long threatened by your sternness,
May dreamlessly join hands
To dance and sing
'What holy changes,
What nearer distances!'?

THE WORDS

That hag with you there
Has such intelligence
You slit her tongue.
Keep her by you,
Don't be alone
Or search for other
Companions now:
She plays cards better
Than you in your patience
And by not saying
She is not what she is
Startles your care:
What lucky wildness –
Look. You've destroyed
What might have come out!
Patience in you
Is a game for two
And the game is cruel
For it cannot end
Because it must end
When her sewn member,
Which cannot speak,
Wags words through a shriek.

SPEECH FROM A PLAY

Helljoy. When I remark or leer, your eyes
Turn from me, wish neither to curb nor to advise
My different sidle-up from yours, my shut
Grave veering towards the green of life. So lamps
Hung out by you dot all my darkness here:
Thus, if I see a deep green floodlit somewhere,
Which tempts my heart, you frame urgent laws
And having checked me, analyse the cause. . . .
Or else it was some tricked-up garden of your own –
A painted cloth explorable by eyes alone.
I am your subject still. All my paths are cut;
None of my letters travels without stamps.
But while you meet to swearing ban the sea
Or hold committees none of you must miss
You'll think of me: I do not mutter emptily
In these deserted streets: *I'll get you for this.*

QUESTIONS BEFORE PARTING

Have you been the victim of a mistake?
Am I dismissed? At noon I must leave
For Gollemburg, from thence entraining
To the University at Wiesenbahr.
When honourably I've acquired my scar
I shall, like other players, stroll aimless,
Cane hung like a sword from twirling fingers,
As symbol of controlled and practised hate
Along the promenades of Europe's spas –
Building the grim legend of one whose skill
In love and death were equalled only
By his heroic and concealed despair.
The object is: you'll hear. Perhaps I'll come
To you, an errant visitor, drink all
Your whisky, go to sleep on your divan.
Will you say you remember me?

But at this moment, as the time draws near
For my departure, it would be easier
To distract your gaze from birds wheeling
In hundreds against a washed-out sky
By rolling my eyes, gesticulating
In a dying agony (look at me now!)
Than to tell you, as I watch your pale lips,
Face grave in its frame of hair,
That I wish you to say
'I must come with you, even to Gollemburg,
So that I could answer with a new smile
'You have asked to come with me, so now
I can stay.'

IN MEMORIAM
Brian Higgins
1930–1965

I sit wanting
You to come in
Remembering
How many times
I turned you out
Busy with stuff
On 'books and life'
Or teaching Arabs
About how to use
Short sentences
(Of which you proved
The better master)
And regretting
I thus betrayed
Your need and trust
But knowing you
Understood
Until with all
Guilt assuaged
Bored with my grief
I read the words
Of poems you wrote
And you are here,
No northern ghost
But my friend still
In your own voice.

BEACH, 1737

Beach, poetical Wrexham wine-merchant,
Your *Eugenio* was unremembered
(Despite the dedication to Pope,
The kindly letter from Jonathan Swift)
From the day it appeared, until this moment.
That year, you cut your throat, suffering
From 'a terrible disorder of the head';
But doubtless you knew a fine rescuing Margoose
Before madness finally had you dead.

Hero, now, of one man's melancholy day:
For you I sheath and dispose the keen carver,
Shut all scissors dangerously open,
Coil and neatly tie the hanging rope,
Begging that if darkness must press on me
And serenity quite withdraw its gift,
I shall lie still, and not become madder –
Rising frenetically up to reach
For the knives I have so quietly put away,
Or rushing to dance in the tempting noose.

But your death had its victory, Beach:
Who now can be sure if the bladed sliver
Not yet smashed out of his perfect windscreen,
The high step crumbling on his sturdy ladder,
The death-claw in his excellent machine,
Are not secret wishes, sharply to end
A peace that sanities merely pretend?

TUTHILL'S ENORMITIES

'. . . [I desire] . . . William Mason, and . . . the Reverend Mr James Browne . . . to apply the sum of two hundred pounds to an use of charity concerning which I have already informed them.'

Thomas Gray's will

'This day the Master in the presence of the Fellows, declared Mr Tuthill's fellowship to be vacant, he having been absent. . . . Since Mr Tuthill's absence common fame has laid him under violent suspicion of having been guilty of great enormities; to clear himself from which he has not made his appearance, and there is good reason to believe he never will.'

Entrances in the college register
of Pembroke Hall, Cambridge, 1756

Through disaster I turn poet monthly
Until your shocked charity redeems me,
Pushing clean despair a step enough away.
A packet from England arrived today
By your kindness, with the usual remittance.
Again I burn all. How many foul true odes
Have thus by generosity been checked?

It's quiet here. On some late evenings
The clouds glow like an orange at High Table
In a silver dish. I have some studies
Of God, who knows how every sparrow falls,
To which to apply my too bored intellect.
With no cash, no influence, I share your view
That I can never again be seen by you.
Not many will ever want to solve
The mystery, *What happened to Tuthill?*

I want now only to give my thanks to Gray,
Tell simply what the burnt odes tried to say:

That I loved best one summer afternoon,
A clean-limbed boy, to whom I'd passed all things
On loveliness that my correctitude
Could bear. But while I spoke of ancient codes
Of classic perfection, the glory of Greece,
Of the gentlest ways to wisdom and peace,
My hand, it seemed like God's, sought out
Despair. Just in that private minute
I could believe that lust and virtue mixed,
That hell and heaven by love are fixed.

Here by your leave, waiting for distant death,
I could have a boy, no question asked,
Could laugh at what you miss in Cambridge,
And send the cynical ones a greeting;
Exchange vile letters, though never meeting.
Why instead should memory shake my foolish frame
With unholy contradictions?
Still timid, I drink wine in careful measures,
Maintain a dignity where no one cares,
Give my desires no hell-won rein:
Remember only shared sunlight, friendship,
The womanless fields beneath the arched blue sky,
And the sweetness of my truest lie
Breathed through the first and ultimate kiss:
'*It's always innocent, just like this!*'

That I loved best one summer afternoon,
A clean-limbed cat, to whom I'd passed all things
[illegible] that for centuries
Could hear. For while I spoke of ancient poets
Of classic perfection [illegible] in Greece,
Of the [illegible] ways in wisdom and peace
My head, a scented [illegible] sought out
[illegible] the private minute
I could believe that just and virtue indeed,
That hell and heaven as here are found.

Here let your leave, waiting for distant death,
Could [illegible], the question asked
Could [illegible] what can [illegible]
[illegible]
Knowing [illegible] never [illegible]
Were [illegible] hand should [illegible] shake my molten frame
With [illegible]
Still hold, I shall smile, [illegible]
[illegible]
[illegible]
Remember only [illegible] sunlight, [illegible]
The [illegible] bridge [illegible] arched blue sky
And [illegible]
[illegible]
[illegible]

IN THE HOTEL

I climbed to the Fifth up the dangerous tube
Footstraps dissolving The friendly dancer
Went off at a tangent safely where her floor led
I called *This is not my herringbone coat*
Folded it gave it to her to return
To the man who'd placed it on my shoulders like a cloak.

Then climbing was easier.

Back on the Ground
                                        Sitting in bed with my mother-wife
                                                                                    You

My wife came in with a double toy-house
One side acid
                    the other sweetmeats
And you offered me my mummified self
Which swallowed, I woke

THE SHORE

Somewhere great life streams choicelessly
Beneath the indifferent, cheerful sun;
But wisely I am here, on a grief-dark shore,
Where fishes in cold sand rot saltily
And uncertain nature pullulates
Gently towards its origin, the sea –
Defeating its preservative
To seek sure, spiritless eternity.

My head is sick, hands deathwards reach.
But despair, hope's wine that ripened
In sun that shone here once before,
Mars carelessly the eager quest.

Even these numb gulpings of oblivion
Are uneasy, and drunkenly transform
The ignorant metaphor.